# STAMPS
## AND STAMP COLLECTING

**Judy Allen**

**Edited by Susan Meredith**

**Designed by Iain Ashman and Graham Round**

**Illustrated by Graham Smith**

**Special consultants: National Postal Museum, London, and Douglas Muir**

## Contents

Most of the stamps in this book are shown actual size. Unused stamps reproduced actual size have to have a band across one corner. This is a postal regulation and the band is not part of the design.

TIGER BOOKS INTERNATIONAL

# Starting a stamp collection

This book will give you a practical introduction to stamps, with lots of ideas on how to start your own collection. You can find out about the different types of stamp, what makes them interesting or valuable, and how they are made, and you can get ideas on how best to collect and arrange your own stamps.

Stamp collecting does not have to be a very expensive hobby. You can ask other people to save their stamps for you and the small amount of basic equipment you need is fairly cheap. What is more, if you build up a good collection, there is always a chance that it will be valuable one day.

When you first start out, it is a good idea to collect all the stamps that come your way. Later, when you have got a better idea of what is available, you can specialize in whatever sort of stamp collecting or "philately" appeals to you most. Here are a few examples.

You can collect the stamps of only certain countries, or of just one country. This is called country-by-country collecting. The stamps here are German.

You can specialize in stamps showing a particular theme or topic, for example, sport. This is known as thematic or topical collecting.

## Where to get stamps

Start off by saving whatever stamps come on your own or your family's mail, and ask other people if they will save theirs for you. People who get a lot of mail from abroad or who work for companies which do business abroad can be especially helpful. Explain to people that it is important to cut stamps off envelopes without damaging them, or ask them to give you the whole envelope if they can.

If you are collecting stamps from your own country, you can save up and buy all the ones that are currently available from the post office.

To get your collection started, it is worth buying a cheap pack of stamps from a toyshop, stationer's or stamp shop. Some contain stamps from all over the world, some from just one country and others have stamps on a theme. Beware though. The stamps may have been stuck to a backing with glue and so will not be in very good condition. Don't buy a pack from the window, as sunlight can fade the colours.

To get a particular stamp, you will probably have to buy from a stamp dealer. You will find dealers' advertisements in stamp magazines

## Equipment

Here is the basic stamp collecting equipment you will need. ▶

Stamp hinges for sticking stamps in your album.

Magnifying glass for studying details.

Album or stock book to keep your stamps in.

Tweezers for handling stamps without damaging them or getting them dirty. Use proper stamp tweezers with rounded ends; ones with sharp ends can pierce a stamp.

Pen for writing notes in your album.

and it is often possible to buy from them by post.

Some firms send out stamps on approval for you to select the ones you want and return the rest, enclosing payment. Always send the stamps back within the specified time limit or you may have to pay

for the whole lot.

If you have friends who collect stamps or if you join a club (see page 30), you can swap duplicate stamps with other people. Make sure that two stamps really are the same before you swap and always keep the one which is in better condition.

**3**

Some people collect only first day covers. These are special envelopes sold by the post office or stamp shops on the day new stamps are authorized for use. You stick the new stamps on and post the envelope to yourself.

**4**

You can specialize in certain types of stamp. The ones shown here are called commemoratives because they celebrate a particular event or anniversary.

**5**

You may find you become as interested in the postmarks that go with stamps as in the stamps themselves. Collecting postmarks is a specialized branch of philately.

## Albums

There is a vast range of albums to choose from. All the types shown here come in a wide variety of prices.

Country-by-country album with printed likenesses of some stamps. Quite useful for beginners.

Loose-leaf album, blank except for grid. Good for thematic collectors and anyone who wants to organize their collection exactly how they please.

Loose-leaf country-by-country album with printed page headings. Useful for country-by-country collectors who want to design their own page layout.

Rings mean the album lies flat when open, and you can take pages out or buy new ones and add them.

First day cover album with transparent polythene pockets.

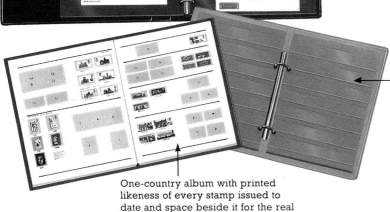

One-country album with printed likeness of every stamp issued to date and space beside it for the real stamp. For one-country specialists.

Stock book with transparent pockets across page. This is not an album but is useful if you have not decided how to organize your collection.

## Catalogues

To identify and study your stamps, and to find out what others are available, you can look at a catalogue. Ones published by the major dealers give details of every stamp ever issued. You should be able to look at an up-to-date edition in a library. You can find out how to use a catalogue on page 29.

## Making notes

You may want to write a few notes in your album beside the stamps and, if your album is blank, you can write in your own page headings. You can use a pen (ones with quick drying ink are best) or pencil. If your handwriting is not very neat, it can be a good idea to use a typewriter, or stencils, which you can buy from a stationer's or toyshop. Some stamp shops sell gummed strips with the names of countries on them.

# Types of stamp

Here are some examples of the different types of stamp you will come across. You will find that most fit into more than one category: for example, the Italian definitive below is now obsolete, the San Marino air mail is also a commemorative and almost all the stamps shown here are pictorial.

## Definitives

Swiss stamp.

Definitives are the "everyday" stamps of a country and often keep the same design for several years. They are issued in denominations to cover all the postal needs of the issuing country and each denomination is usually in different colours.

## Pictorials

A pictorial is any stamp which has a picture on it. Most stamps designed today are pictorials, though you will come across definitives with an abstract design (the Swiss one shown on the left, for example) and many obsolete stamps have no picture on them.

## Commemoratives

1879-1979 Nederland 45c

Commemoratives are issued in honour of an anniversary or special event and are available for a limited time only. The purpose of issue usually appears on them.

## Special issues

Photography USA 15c

Special issues are not tied to a specific event and there is often no purpose of issue shown on them. Like commemoratives, they are available for a limited time.

## Air mails

Some countries, especially those which carry some of their internal mail by air, issue special air mail stamps. To find out more about air mail, see page 26.

## Charity stamps

Charity stamps are sold at a higher price than their postal value and the difference goes to the relevant charity. Usually, the amount which is to go to charity and, often, the type of charity are shown on the stamp as well as the postal rate.

## Obsoletes

These are out-of-date stamps. They may be from a country which still issues stamps, such as Austria or Japan, or from a "dead country": that is one that has changed its name, such as Tanganyika, or is now part of another country, such as Bavaria.

## Coils

Perforations

Slot machines contain special coils of stamps. The stamps often have no perforations either at the sides or at the top and bottom.

## Stamps on postal stationery

Postal stationery usually has stamps printed on it. If the stamps are cut off the stationery and stuck on an ordinary letter they are still valid. This kite is a stamp on a Swedish aerogramme.

## Locals

Local stamps are only valid within one district or town and are usually issued by civic authorities, private firms or landowners. It is best to keep them on a separate page from the stamps in your main collection.

## Special purpose stamps

These include stamps like the postage due, certified mail (recorded delivery), government and military stamps shown above. Special purpose stamps are often listed in catalogues at the end of a country's entry. Like locals, it is best to keep them separate from your main collection.

## Bogus stamps

The stamp above is bogus and has no postal value at all. Bogus stamps are sometimes produced for propaganda purposes but more often to fool collectors. They often have the names of non-existent countries on them. If you cannot identify a stamp after a thorough search through the catalogues, there is always the chance it may be bogus.

## Mint and used stamps

Used stamp

Mint stamp

A mint stamp is one which has never been through the post and is in perfect condition, whereas a used stamp has been posted. Used stamps are not necessarily worth less than mint stamps provided they are in good condition. This means they must not be dirty, creased or torn (always check carefully for damaged perforations) and the postmark should not be too heavy or cover up an important part of the design.

## Harmful or improper issues

This is the title for stamps blacklisted by the Fédération Internationale de Philatelie (F.I.P.). The stamps are not bogus, because they are valid for carrying mail, but they are issued solely with collectors in mind rather than to meet a postal need. Often they are of high denominations and have pictures which do not relate to the country of issue.

There is nothing to stop you collecting these stamps but they are not usually worth much and, if you entered them in a competition, they would lose you marks. Stamp magazines often give information about banned issues and reputable dealers will advise you.

Watch out too for stamps which have been "cancelled to order". This means they have been postmarked but not sent through the post. They are often sold at a reduced price to the makers of cheap packs. Look out for stamps with a very neat, clear cancellation in one corner and also check for gum on a postmarked stamp.

# Handling and studying stamps

## Taking stamps off envelopes

**1**

Start by cutting neatly around the stamp, not so close to the perforations that you damage them. If a stamp has an interesting postmark, either leave it on its envelope or cut out the stamp and postmark together and put them in your album like that. Never remove stamps from a first day cover.

**2**

Tearing or steaming stamps off an envelope can damage them. Float them face up in a bowl of clean, lukewarm water for about 20 minutes. Try not to let water get on the face of the stamps: the ink on some stamps may run. Float stamps on coloured envelopes separately in case the colour runs and spoils the others.

**3**

Gently peel the paper from the stamp, not the stamp from the paper. If the two don't come apart easily, float them for a while longer. This is the only time you should use your hands, not tweezers, to handle stamps. Tweezers can damage a wet stamp.

## Storing stamps

**1**

The cheapest way of storing stamps until you are ready to put them in your album is to keep them in clean envelopes. Sort the stamps according to how you plan to arrange your album. If, for example, you are going to make a country-by-country collection, just write the name of the country on each envelope and stack them in a box.

**2**

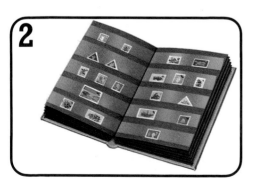

If you prefer, you can buy a stock book. These have transparent strips across the pages and stamps can be slipped in and out easily.

## Close-up of a stamp

Country of issue · Margin · Borderline · Design · Portrait of head of state

Designer's name · Purpose of issue · Perforation hole · Perforation tooth · Printer's name · Denomination

The labels to the enlarged stamp above show you the names of the different parts of a stamp. All stamps have some of the things shown on this one, but very few have all of them. Some have no margin or borderline.

Some have no portrait. Some do not give the name of the designer or printer. And, by tradition, British stamps never state their country of issue in words but just show the monarch's head.

## 4

Wash off any traces of surplus gum with a paintbrush, or old toothbrush, dipped in clean, lukewarm water.

## 5

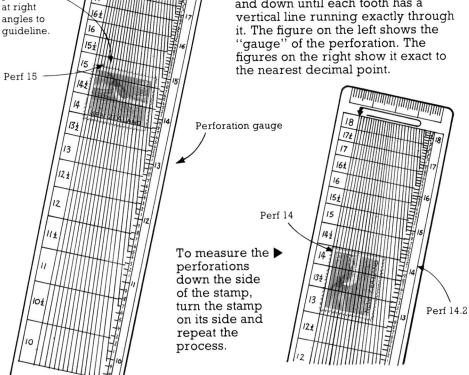

Spread the stamps, face down, on a piece of clean, absorbent paper to dry. Use white blotting paper, white kitchen towel or white soft toilet paper. To stop them curling up, put another piece of the paper on top and a heavy book on top of that. Never dry stamps in sunlight or near heat: they will curl up.

## Looking more closely

There are several more advanced pieces of equipment you can buy from stamp shops and some stationers' to help you study your stamps in more detail. Here are some examples of the less expensive things.

A colour guide helps you to identify the colours described in catalogues and to tell the difference between ones that sound the same, such as red, crimson and vermilion.

You may also be able to tell from a colour guide if the colour of a reprinted stamp has varied slightly from the original. If only a few are printed in one shade, they may be more valuable than the rest.

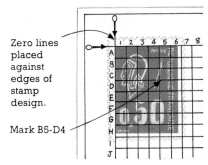

Zero lines placed against edges of stamp design.

Mark B5-D4

A position finder helps you to note the position of a mark or flaw if you are buying, selling or enquiring about a stamp by post. Put the position finder on top of the stamp with the zero lines against the edges of the stamp design. Then you can note the position of any detail by reading off the letter and figure of the square it is in.

Some watermarks (see page 16) show if you hold the stamp up to a strong light. Hidden watermarks should show up for a moment if you spray watermark fluid on to the back of the stamp. The fluid comes in aerosol cans. It is usually inflammable, so follow the instructions carefully.

## Measuring perforations

Perforations are the small holes between stamps which help you tear them apart. Two stamps which look alike may have perforations of different sizes.

If a catalogue lists a stamp as *Perf 13*, that means it has 13 complete perforations (teeth plus holes) in every two centimetres. If the top measure is different from the side, the top number is written first: *Perf 13 x 14*, for example.

If the stamp is not too small, you can measure two centimetres with a ruler and then count the perforations, but it is easier, and not expensive, to buy a transparent perforation gauge and use that.

◀ Put the gauge over the stamp, keeping the guideline on the left at right angles to the row of perforations you are measuring. Slide the gauge up and down until each tooth has a vertical line running exactly through it. The figure on the left shows the "gauge" of the perforation. The figures on the right show it exact to the nearest decimal point.

Guideline

Row of perforations at right angles to guideline.

Perf 15

Perforation gauge

Perf 14

To measure the ▶ perforations down the side of the stamp, turn the stamp on its side and repeat the process.

Perf 14.2

# Collecting by country

The most traditional way of grouping stamps is into countries, with each country being given a separate section of the album. The list on pages 28–29 of this book will help you identify which countries your stamps are from.

After a while, you will probably find that you want to specialize in the stamps of just one or two countries: those whose stamps you particularly like or can most easily get hold of. Specializing is also the best way of building up a collection of any value.

Before you begin, it is a good idea to glance through a catalogue to see roughly how many stamps are available. Have a look at the dealers' prices quoted, then you can decide which stamps you can afford to buy and which ones it is worth leaving space for in your album in case you might get them in the future.

It is usual to mount stamps in a country-by-country collection in chronological order, always keeping sets together and mounting mint stamps separately from used. When you are starting out, you may prefer to reverse the order and mount the most recent stamps first, as these are the ones you are most likely to get. Then you can work backwards.

## Stamps from your own country

It is usually easiest to obtain stamps from your own country. As well as collecting any that come through the mail, you can save up and buy all the stamps available from the post office, adding new issues as they appear, and gradually getting hold of older stamps.

Even within one country, you may eventually decide to restrict your collection to stamps issued over a limited period, say, within the last twenty years, or since the year you were born. If a country has a monarch or president, it is possible to make a "single reign" or "single presidency" collection. The British stamps on the right have all been issued in the reign of Elizabeth II.

## Name changes

Try and be aware of countries changing their names, like Zimbabwe (formerly Rhodesia) and Sri Lanka (formerly Ceylon). You may want to collect the stamps of the new country only or of the old one too.

## Places with links

Once you have chosen a country, you can decide whether to include in your collection stamps from small areas which have close ties with it. For example, an Australian collection could include the stamps above.

## Bilinguals

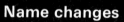

Look out for stamps which have printing in two or, as in the case of the Swiss stamp above, three languages. This means that the different languages are spoken in the country of issue. Some countries print different stamps for each of the languages.

## Learning about countries

You can often learn quite a lot about a country from what is shown on its stamps: its crops, industries, famous people, works of art, landscape and wildlife, for example. Take care, though. The iguana on the Fijian stamp above is shown not because it is a common animal there but because it is in danger of dying out.

## Joint issues

Sometimes countries produce stamps with the same design to indicate a special link between them or to celebrate a joint achievement. The U.S.A. and U.S.S.R. issued the stamps shown below to commemorate the link-up in space of the Apollo and Soyuz satellites.

## Sets

A set is a number of ▶ related stamps in a series of denominations issued at the same time or within a period. Some, including many definitive sets, have the same design but different colours for each denomination. Others, like the set on the right, are all on one theme but have a different design for each denomination. You will find that most dealers do not like to sell individual stamps from a set.

## Booklets

Booklets of stamps ▶ were introduced as a convenience, but have now become "collectables" and there are special albums for them. They usually contain definitives.

Utgivningsdag: 8 oktober 1977
Foto: Lars Söderbom, Anders Florén
Gravörer: Zlatko Jakus, Martin Mörck
Omslag: Jan Magnusson

## Miniature sheets

These are issued solely for collectors. They consist of one or more stamps and a border, which often has illustrations relevant to the issue, as on the sheet above. The stamps are postally valid.

## Supranationals

A few international organizations, including the ones named on the stamps above, have the right to issue their own stamps. These can be bought in places where the organizations have head offices and are valid to carry mail world wide. Keep stamps like these separate from your main collection.

# Arranging and mounting

Your stamps will look best if you don't crowd too many on one page and if you keep your arrangement simple. Always try and decide where you want to put all the stamps on a page before you start mounting them. Use the grid of faint, printed squares on the page to help you get them straight and evenly spaced, and make a faint pencil mark where each one is to go.

Always make any notes before you start mounting, to avoid damaging the stamps. Full details would include the date of issue, reason for issue, names of designer and printer, printing process and perforation gauge. You can get this information from catalogues, but don't be tempted to make too many notes or they will spoil the look of the page. It is a good idea to write your notes out neatly on a piece of scrap paper first, to see exactly how much space they take up.

This page from an album shows you how stamps can be arranged.

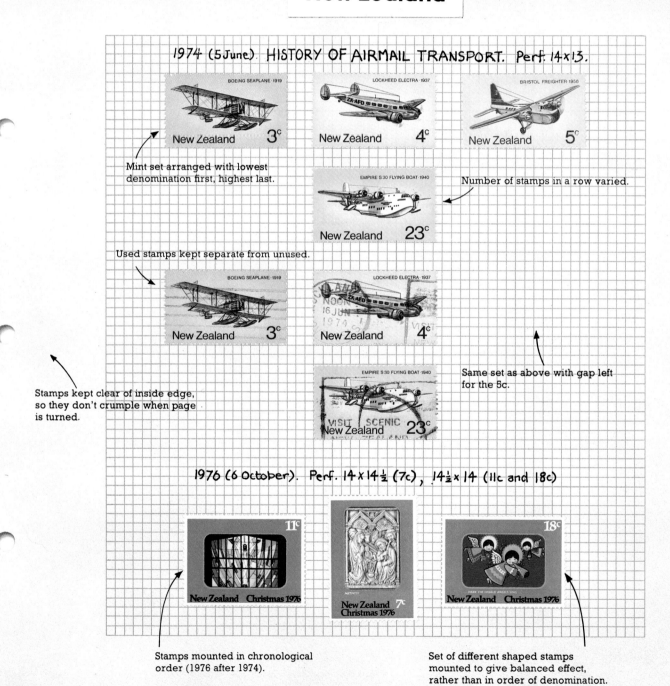

Plenty of space for heading. →

**New Zealand**

1974 (5 June). HISTORY OF AIRMAIL TRANSPORT. Perf. 14×13.

Mint set arranged with lowest denomination first, highest last.

Number of stamps in a row varied.

Used stamps kept separate from unused.

Same set as above with gap left for the 5c.

Stamps kept clear of inside edge, so they don't crumple when page is turned.

1976 (6 October). Perf. 14×14½ (7c), 14½×14 (11c and 18c)

Stamps mounted in chronological order (1976 after 1974).

Set of different shaped stamps mounted to give balanced effect, rather than in order of denomination.

## Using stamp hinges

Always use proper stamp hinges to mount your stamps. If you use sticky tape, pieces of stamp edging or the gum on the stamp itself, you will damage the stamp and reduce its value.

Most hinges are ready folded. If yours are not, fold over about the top quarter, sticky side out. Make sure you fold straight or the stamp will not lie straight on the page.

**2**

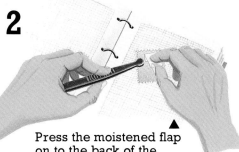

Press the moistened flap on to the back of the stamp, near the top but clear of the perforations.

**4**

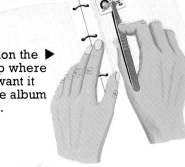

Position the ▶ stamp where you want it on the album page.

**1**

Use the ▶ tip of your tongue or lick your finger to moisten the flap slightly.

**3**

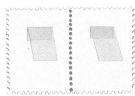

Then moisten a strip across the bottom of ◀ the hinge.

**5**

◀ Put a sheet of clean paper over the stamp and press it gently so the hinge sticks to the page.

## Unusual shaped stamps

Mount a pair of ▶ stamps like this, keeping the hinges clear of the perforations between the two.

Mount a triangle like this, with ▲ the hinge on the side nearest the centre of the album so the stamp will not get crumpled when the album is shut.

For a very small stamp, ▶ cut a hinge in half, lengthways or widthways, depending on the shape.

If you have a block of stamps, don't tear them apart. Mount them together, using as many hinges as are necessary to fix the block securely. ▼

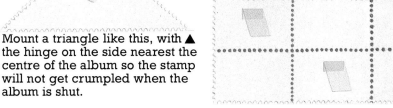

## Mint stamps

Strip mount

A hinge will leave a faint mark on the back of a mint stamp and this can reduce its value. So, if you have a valuable mint stamp, it is a good idea to use a strip mount, even though these are more expensive than hinges. Moisten the gummed back of the mount, stick it to the page and slip the stamp under the transparent flap at the front. Some people use strip mounts for all mint stamps.

## First day covers

If you want to keep first day covers in an ordinary stamp album, you can mount them with transparent photograph corners.

## Moving stamps

If you mount a stamp in the wrong place, or get it crooked, wait for at least half an hour until the gum on the hinge has completely dried. Then the hinge will peel off the page and off the stamp without doing any damage. This means you can also take stamps out of your album to rearrange, sell or swap.

# Collecting by theme

If you don't want to group your stamps by country, you can sort them according to the subjects of the pictures shown on them. The number of topics shown on stamps is almost endless, so you should have no difficulty in finding ones you are interested in.

Before you start to specialize in a theme, have a look through a whole-world catalogue to get a rough idea of how many appropriate stamps there are and whether you could afford them. To find out exactly what stamps are available on a particular subject, you could go right through the catalogue, page by page, noting down the ones that were relevant.

There are no theme catalogues, but the American Topical Association (address on page 30) publishes handbooks and checklists of all the stamps there are on the most popular topics, such as the ones shown on these pages.

Below are some examples of stamps on just a few of the possible subjects you could choose for a thematic collection.

# Organizing a thematic collection

Once you have collected a number of stamps on one subject, you will need to decide how to arrange them. Most broad topics can be broken down quite easily. For example, transport can be divided into groups including cars, trains, planes, boats and ships, and a collection on sport can be divided into different sports.

Below is a possible breakdown for a theme on wildlife. You could mount each of the six categories on a separate page of your album. You may eventually decide to specialize in only one or two of the categories.

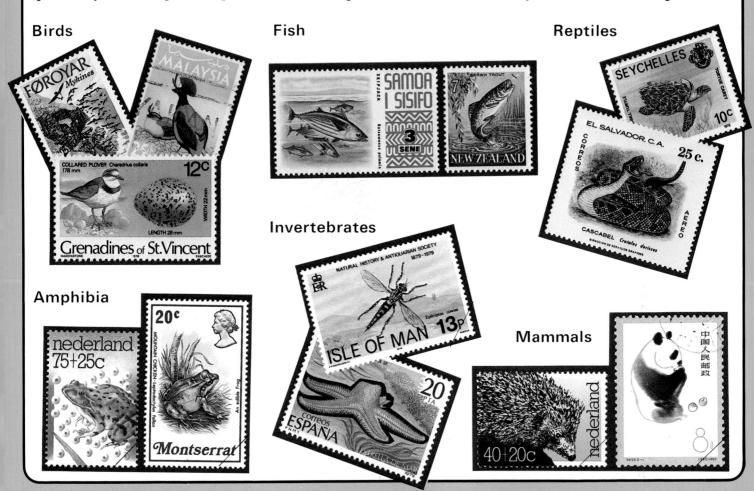

## Birds

## Fish

## Reptiles

## Invertebrates

## Amphibia

## Mammals

---

If you got too many stamps on any of the categories above for one page, you could subdivide them. Mammals, for instance, would divide into groups including those shown here. Looking at books on wildlife would help you find out more about these and other groups.

**Primates** (including monkeys and humans)

**Carnivores** (including cats, dogs, bears and badgers)

**Rodents** (including squirrels, rats and mice)

**Ungulates** (including horses, rhinos, pigs, deer and cattle)

---

You could go even further and break, say, horses down into different groups.

## Horses

Racing horses

Horses from legend and history.

Working horses

# More about collecting by theme

## Looking closely

If you are hunting for stamps to fit into a particular theme, get into the habit of looking very closely at all the stamps you get. It is easy to overlook a small detail which would justify a stamp being included in your collection: for example, the bird in the stamp above.

Could go in animals, children or literature.

This is a concert hall, so could go in music. Also architecture.

These are feathers, so could go in birds as well as costume.

Ginseng, so could go in herbs or medicine as well as plants or flowers.

It is often hard to tell exactly what a stamp is showing and so what theme you could put it in. Looking it up in a catalogue will help you to find out. Most stamps, including the ones shown above, will fit into more than one theme.

## Purpose of issue collecting

Instead of collecting stamps on a particular subject, you can collect stamps issued for a certain purpose: usually commemoratives. Here are some examples.

Every time the Olympic Games are held, lots of countries issue commemorative stamps. ▶

◀ Because there are now so many Olympic stamps, you might eventually decide to restrict your collection to just one or two sports within the Games.

Since 1959 there have been world "years" announced by the United Nations and many countries issue commemorative stamps. You could make a general collection of these stamps, or try collecting every stamp commemorating a particular year. These stamps were issued for the "year of the child". ▼

It is possible to build up a large collection of stamps issued specially to commemorate the postal services. Hundreds of stamps have been issued in honour of the Englishman, Rowland Hill, who introduced the first adhesive postage stamp in 1840. ▼

## Telling a story with stamps

You can collect and arrange stamps so that they trace the historical development of something, for example, inventions and discoveries, different kinds of transport, the postal services.

It is best to plan out your story quite carefully before you start. By going through a catalogue, you will find out which stamps you could use to tell your story and you can decide how complete you want the story to be.

The story of flight shown below is very brief. There are many other stamps which you could use to tell the same story and many you could use to make it longer.

It is not always necessary to put the stamps in strict historical order, even when you are telling a story. The shape of the stamps and the overall look of the page still have to be taken into account, and, by grouping certain stamps together, you can emphasize parts of your story.

Any notes you make can draw attention to the parts of the stamps' pictures which best illustrate the story.

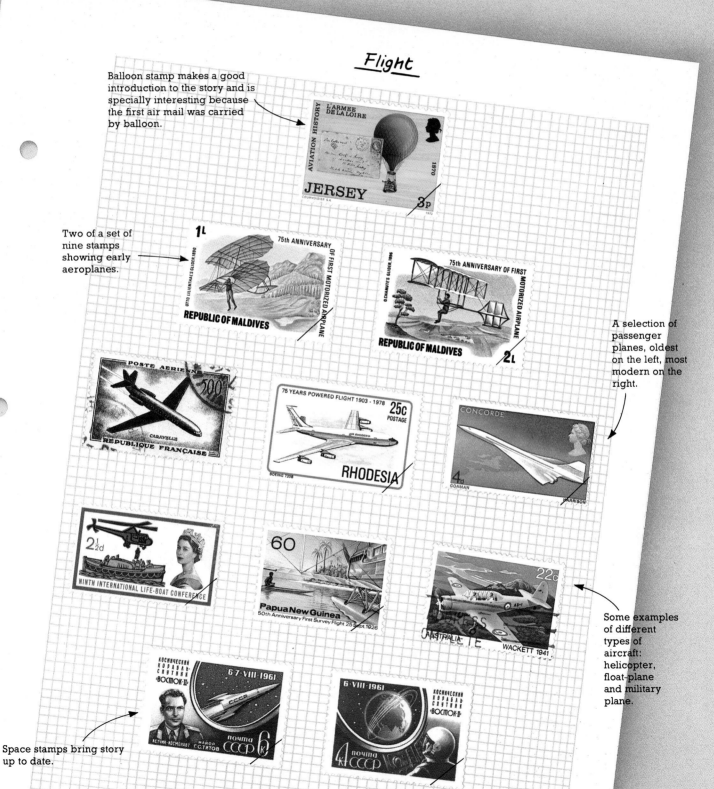

*Flight*

Balloon stamp makes a good introduction to the story and is specially interesting because the first air mail was carried by balloon.

Two of a set of nine stamps showing early aeroplanes.

A selection of passenger planes, oldest on the left, most modern on the right.

Some examples of different types of aircraft: helicopter, float-plane and military plane.

Space stamps bring story up to date.

15

# How stamps are made

## 1

Two proposed designs for the same stamp, both of which were reduced to actual size.

Unaccepted design

Accepted design

When a new stamp is needed, the post office commissions a number of designs. These are usually produced four times bigger than the required size. When one of the designs has been selected, it is reduced photographically to the right size.

## 2

When stamp is magnified, dots show up.

The finished design is photographed several times through different coloured filters, so that each time only one colour is picked up. It is also photographed through a fine screen or mesh, so that the picture is broken up into lots of minute dots. If you look at a printed stamp through a strong magnifying glass, you can sometimes see the different coloured dots.

## How the colours build up

First cylinder prints yellow.

Second cylinder prints red (called "magenta") on top.

Third cylinder adds blue (called "cyan").

Fourth cylinder prints black on top.

These stamps were produced specially to show how the different colours build up, one on top of the other, as the printing cylinders come into contact with the paper. Ignore the top part of the stamps where there is writing and just look at the pictures. The picture on the bottom right is made up of just four colours. Sometimes, for more richly coloured stamps, machines with seven or more cylinders are used.

## Printers' marks

RED ADMIRAL

12p

BAILIWICK of GUERNSEY

1B    1B    1B    1B

HARRISON & SONS LIMITED

Number of one of plates or cylinders used to print stamps.

Name of printer

Blobs of colour, often called "traffic lights", show which colour inks were used to print the stamps.

"Register marks" like this help the printer keep the paper straight as it goes through the machine, so that each colour falls in exactly the right place.

When you get stamps from the edge of a sheet, you will often see printers' marks, like these, in the margin. It can be interesting to collect them.

## Watermarks

Lesotho watermark in shape of Basuto hat.

Dandy roll

Bits

Jamaican "J" and pineapple watermark.

Sometimes stamp paper has a watermark in it to make forgery more difficult. The mark is pressed into the paper by "bits" of metal arranged in a specific pattern and attached to a cylinder or "dandy roll", which is passed over the paper while it is being made.

**3**

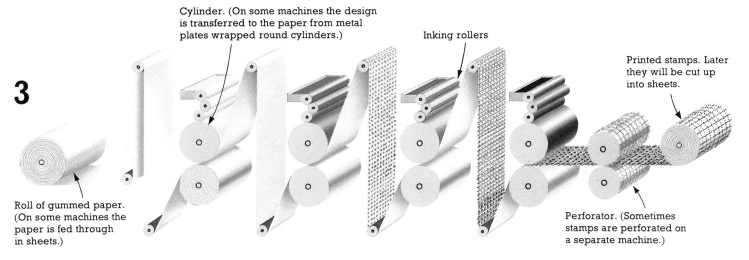

Cylinder. (On some machines the design is transferred to the paper from metal plates wrapped round cylinders.)

Inking rollers

Printed stamps. Later they will be cut up into sheets.

Roll of gummed paper. (On some machines the paper is fed through in sheets.)

Perforator. (Sometimes stamps are perforated on a separate machine.)

These dotted photographs are then transferred by means of chemicals to a series of metal "plates" or cylinders: one for each colour. Here is a very simplified picture of a fast, modern type of printing machine which has four cylinders. Each cylinder is inked with a different colour and gummed stamp paper is passed through the machine. It goes round each cylinder in turn, and the design is transferred from the cylinders to the paper, one colour at a time. This machine also perforates the stamps.

## Different types of printing

You will see the names of several different printing processes in stamp catalogues. All of them fall into one of these three main categories.

**1 Recess printing**

Design is recessed.

The design is "etched" or sunk below the surface of the printing plate or cylinder. The ink collects in the recesses and, when the plate comes into contact with the paper, the design is transferred. You can feel slight ridges on the front of some recess printed stamps. Recess printing is sometimes called intaglio. Photogravure and line engraving are both types of recess printing.

**3 Lithography**

Design is flat.

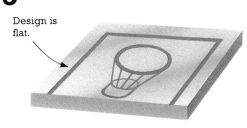

In this method, the printing plate is completely flat but it is treated with special chemicals so that the ink will settle only on the parts of the design which are to be printed. You cannot feel any ridges on stamps printed by lithography. Offset lithography is a more complicated form of this process.

**2 Letterpress**

Design is raised.

In this process, the blank parts of the design are recessed, leaving the areas which are to be printed slightly raised. Ink is spread on the raised areas only and, when contact is made, the design is transferred to the paper. You can sometimes feel slight ridges on the *back* of letterpress printed stamps. Letterpress is also known as relief or surface printing, or typography.

**Embossing**

One plate has design raised.

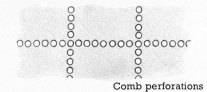

Paper →

One plate has design recessed.

This is a combination of recess and letterpress printing. The paper is sandwiched between two plates, one with the design recessed, the other with the design raised. This makes the design on the stamp noticeably raised. Embossing is a slow and expensive process, generally only used nowadays to print stamps direct on to envelopes.

---

**Making perforations**

Comb punch

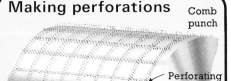

Perforating pins

"Comb" perforating is the method most commonly used today. The perforating pins are arranged so that holes are punched across the tops and bottoms of the stamps at the same time as down the sides.

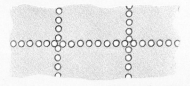

Comb perforations

If you look at a block of stamps which have been comb perforated, you will see that the perforations are neat at the corners.

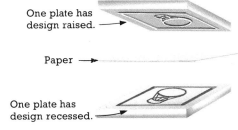

Line perforations

In line perforating, there is a single line of pins and only one row of holes is punched at a time. If you look at a block of line perforated stamps, you will see that the holes do not match perfectly where the lines intersect.

# Unusual stamps

All the stamps on these pages are rather out of the ordinary, though they are not necessarily rare or valuable. You are more likely to come across some of these types of stamp than others. For example, forging and faking have almost died out nowadays and bisects are also rather rare. It is possible to specialize in unusual stamps, or you can just mount any that you come across in the relevant place in your collection.

Stamps sent out to the Universal Postal Union (U.P.U.) or to the press before their official date of issue are overprinted "specimen" so they cannot be used on mail.

Rebel groups sometimes overprint their initials on stamps to get publicity.

If a country changes its name, the new name is often overprinted on existing stamps until new ones can be printed.

## Overprints

You will probably come across stamps which have had extra printing added to them since they were originally printed. There are several reasons for making these "overprints". Here are some examples.

This stamp has the Japanese flag flying at the top of a tower. For political reasons, the issuing country (East China) did not want it to show, so they printed this character over the top.

## Surcharges

An overprint which changes the denomination of a stamp is called a "surcharge". These are used if there is a temporary shortage of stamps of a particular denomination, or if the postage rate changes and new stamps have not been printed (as was the case with these two stamps), or if the currency changes.

## Twins

Keep a look out for "twin" stamps like these. They make a picture when joined together and still make separate pictures when torn apart. Always mount twins unseparated.

## Perfins

Stamps with initials perforated into them are known as "perfins". They usually indicate government use but are sometimes put in by private firms to deter staff from using the stamps on their personal mail. MCBM on the stamp above stands for Mauritius Commercial Bank, Mauritius.

## Bisects

Post offices occasionally allow stamps to be cut in half to halve their value and these are called "bisects". The one above was not authorized but still managed to get through the mail without incurring excess postage. On a few occasions, even "quadrisects" (stamps cut into quarters) have got through.

## Back printing

It is worth glancing at the back of a stamp, just in case there is any printing there. Usually it will be an advertising slogan, like this one promoting tourism in Madeira. It is best to mount stamps like this in the usual way, but you can make a note drawing attention to the back.

18

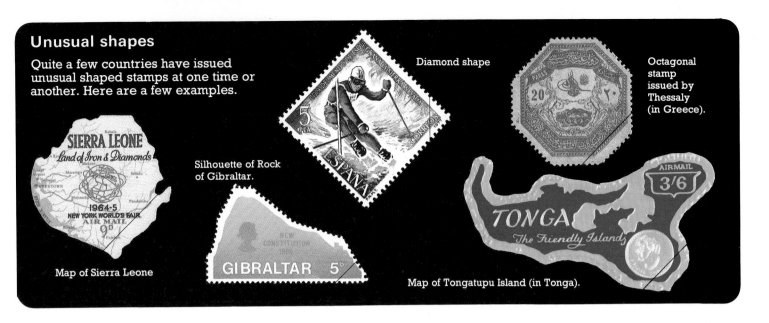

## Unusual shapes

Quite a few countries have issued unusual shaped stamps at one time or another. Here are a few examples.

Map of Sierra Leone

Silhouette of Rock of Gibraltar.

Diamond shape

Octagonal stamp issued by Thessaly (in Greece).

Map of Tongatapu Island (in Tonga).

## Unusual paper

In times of shortage, stamps have been printed on paper normally used for other purposes, including rice paper, newspaper, the back of maps and even school exercise books. This is the back of a Latvian stamp which was printed on the reverse of a half-printed banknote.

## Three-dimensional stamps

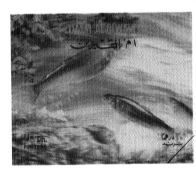

A few countries have experimented recently to produce stamps that look three-dimensional, using a special combination of printing methods. This is an example, though the effect is harder to see here than on the original.

## The smallest and largest stamps

1863 Bolivaran stamp.

1856 Mecklenburg-Schwerin stamps.

Experts disagree about which is the smallest stamp ever produced. Many say it is the Bolivaran stamp above. But, although the stamps from Mecklenburg-Schwerin were only ever sold in groups of four, they could be used singly and one of these is smaller than the stamp from Bolivar.

The largest stamp in the world is the one below, issued by the U.S.A. in 1865 for posting newspapers.

## 1 Forgeries and fakes

Genuine stamp          Forgery

Early stamps were designed in very intricate detail in an attempt to deter forgers. Nevertheless, quite a lot of forgery went on, usually to cheat collectors rather than the post office. See if you can spot any differences between the two stamps here. It is very difficult to detect a good forgery, especially if there are no examples of the genuine stamp at hand for comparison.

## 2

A forgery is a completely new stamp made to look like another one, whereas a fake is an existing stamp which has been tampered with to make it appear more valuable than it is. At one time it was quite common to fake perforations: often by cutting them off, as we have done to this stamp. Sometimes they were added, by means of a small hand perforator, to stamps which were meant to be imperforate.

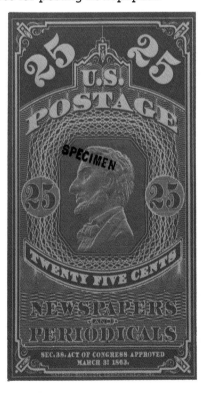

# Mistakes on stamps

Although a damaged stamp loses much of its value unless it is very rare, a stamp with a mistake in its design or printing usually gains, depending on how many were printed with the mistake. The fewer there are, the more valuable they are likely to be.

It is possible to specialize in collecting stamps with errors, though, apart from some common ones, they are expensive to obtain. If you can, it is best always to mount a correct example of the stamp beside the error.

## Errors in design

Stamps are carefully checked at various stages in production but errors made in the original design sometimes slip through. Here are some examples.

This stamp commemorates the death of the composer, Schumann but has music by Schubert in the background. ▶

Jessleton should be spelt Jesselton.

The scaly ant eater cannot walk on two legs, only on all fours. ▼

The sailing canoe should have a helmsman.

◀ The line of latitude should be 49 30′N. 40 30′N runs just north of Madrid, in Spain.

## Printing errors

Stamps are also carefully checked during printing. Any that are found to have mistakes are meant to be destroyed on the spot. Here are some printers' errors that got through.

◀ Sometimes the wrong colour ink is used. The central part of this stamp should be red and black.

◀ Older printing machines could only print one colour at a time, which meant that the paper had to be taken out and fed through the machine several times during the course of printing. Here, the paper was put in the wrong way round for the centre picture to be printed and so it is "inverted" or upside down.

These stamps were overprinted upside down. The bars should have blotted out the value at the top of the stamps. ▶

Train should be red. ⎯

Circle should be red with value printed on in white.

◀ Even on modern, multi-colour machines, it is possible for a colour to be missed out completely, for example, if the ink supply fails. Both these stamps were printed without any red. ▶

Flag should have red cross on it.

## Errors in perforation

When sheets of stamps are trimmed to go in booklets, perforations sometimes get cut off. You may well come across a booklet stamp with perforations cut off on one side, like this one. This is fairly common and is unlikely to make the stamp valuable.

Here the perforator missed its mark and cut through one of the stamps. This is quite a rare mistake and, if the perforations cut right into the design, as they do here, it can make the stamps very valuable.

These two stamps missed out on perforation all together and are rare and valuable. Always try to collect errors like this in pairs to prove you have not cut the perforations off. Bear in mind that some countries issue the same stamp both with and without perforations.

## Deliberate errors

This stamp was issued with the yellow printed upside down. When the United States post office became aware of the error, they printed lots more exactly the same so that the stamp would not be rare and people would be prevented from making money out of their mistake.

## Looking for errors

It is always worth keeping a look out for errors, but beware of finding them where none exist.

A lot of collectors ▶ pounced on these stamps when they were first issued, saying that seals have flippers, not paws. But there was no mistake. These are great grey seals, which have paws at the front.

▲ "Welthy" is not a spelling mistake. Welthy Fisher is the name of the man shown on the top left of this stamp.

## Varieties

A mistake which occurs during printing but only affects one stamp every so often, not the whole batch, is called a variety rather than an error. Varieties are generally considered less serious than errors and you are more likely to find them, as they are often not destroyed. It is interesting to collect them, although they are usually less valuable than errors. Here are some of the types of variety you may come across.

Here a circle got punched out of the margin of the paper and stuck to the cylinder, picking up blue ink. This is known as a "confetti flaw".

The white mark on the stamp above was caused by a tiny piece of dirt on the cylinder preventing the blue ink from printing. Flaws like this are known as "fly specks".

◀ Surplus ink is wiped off the cylinders by means of a "doctor blade". Here, the blade jammed, causing this thin white line to appear across a number of stamps.

# Postmarks

Once you start looking at envelopes for their stamps, you will soon begin to notice interesting postmarks too. As well as collecting any that come on your own or other people's mail, you can get postmarks from some stamp dealers (look for advertisements in the stamp magazines) and, if you join a stamp club, you should be able to get swaps.

The Universal Postal Union (U.P.U.) publishes huge, world-wide directories of post offices, so you can find out what postmarks exist, in the same way that you can find out about stamps from catalogues. Most countries produce their own individual directories.

You should find them in a good reference library.

If you are particularly keen to have the postmark of a certain place, you might get it if you write to the local postmaster. Always remember to enclose return postage (stamps for within your own country or an international reply coupon for countries abroad).

### Bishop marks

Bishop mark dated 1 April.

Postmarks have been in use much longer than stamps. The first officially recognized postmarks were introduced by an Englishman, Henry Bishop, in 1661. They were circular and consisted of the date only. Although they are old, you can buy some bishop marks for only a few pounds.

### Maltese crosses

When stamps were introduced, postmarks had to serve the additional purpose of cancelling the stamps so they could not be reused. The first postmark for a stamp was the Maltese cross, which was introduced in 1840 to cancel Penny Blacks (see page 24).

### Killers

Some of the earliest postmarks were known as "killers" or "obliterators". Here is a killer of the type used in Guernsey in the mid-1870s (the numbers show which post office it was from) and one on a Canadian stamp.

### Modern postmarks

More recent postmarks show the place where the letter was posted, the full date and, often, the time, postcode of the town, number of the post office and post box, and even the number of the machine used to mark the letter.

### Meter marks

Most companies do not put stamps on their mail but frank it with a meter leased from the post office. The meter records the amount of postage used and the firm pays this to the post office in lump sums. You could try building up a collection of meter marks.

### Mobile post offices

Sometimes mail is post-marked not at ordinary post offices but on "mobile post offices" such as trains or buses. The marks above are from a railway post office in New Zealand and a coach post office in Germany.

### Postal slogans

Be on the look out for postmarks which have interesting commemorative or advertising slogans incorporated into them. This French slogan is advertising the town of Pau as a tourist resort.

### Errors in postmarks

You have a chance of finding errors in postmarks just as you do on stamps. This letter was not posted in 1861 but in 1981. The year numbers were put in the cancelling machine upside down. A lot of letters were probably postmarked with this mistake but if most of them get thrown away, this one may become quite rare.

## Organizing a postmark collection

You can organize a collection of postmarks in much the same way as a collection of stamps: for instance, grouping the postmarks into countries and displaying them in alphabetical and date order. You could specialize in the postmarks of certain countries or even of certain towns, especially if you have friends or relations there. Or, you could collect according to the date of the postmark, say from the year when you were born.

On the whole, postmarks do not increase in value as much as stamps, though if you build up a collection over a number of years, it is likely to be worth a reasonable amount.

Below is a selection of postmarks from the island of Jersey and some from different capital cities around the world.

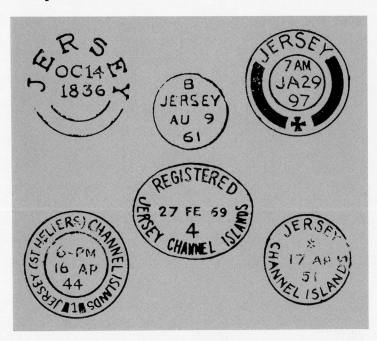

## Displaying postmarks

If you want, you can cut postmarks off their envelopes and mount them in your album like stamps. Remember to cut round the stamp as well as the postmark. Your collection will look neater if you always cut to the same size. 8cm across by 5cm down should be big enough for most postmarks, though for ones with slogans you may need to cut to as much as 10cm by 7cm.

If you have an old or valuable postmark, or, if you are specializing in postmarks, it is best to keep them on their envelopes. You can mount them in a stamp album with photograph corners, like first day covers, or you can buy a special album for them, rather like a first day cover album. Or, if you prefer, you can buy transparent polythene envelopes quite cheaply and store them in those in a cardboard box.

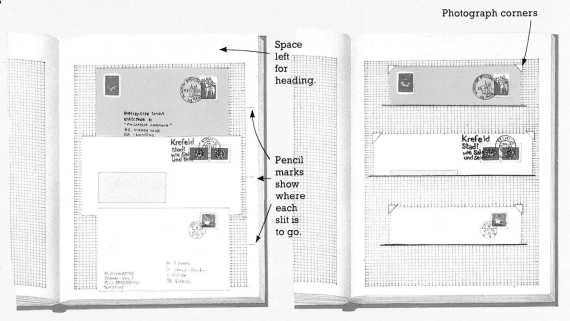

Space left for heading.

Photograph corners

Pencil marks show where each slit is to go.

Another idea is to modify a stamp album by cutting slits across the page, so that you can slide an envelope through each slit until only the section with the postmark is visible.

First, position the envelopes on the page and, allowing space for a heading and any notes, make a faint pencil mark on the page just below the bottom of each postmark. Make sure the bottom envelope is not going to overhang the bottom of the page. Then, using the horizontal grid lines on the page to help you cut straight and the vertical lines to help you get the envelopes central, cut slits across to the width of each envelope. Put the envelopes in the slits and secure the top corners with photograph corners.

# Old, rare and valuable stamps

A Penny Black.

An original Twopenny Blue.

First version of Penny Red.

The first postage stamp with gum on the back was the Penny Black, issued in Great Britain in 1840. Although it was in use for less than a year, several million were printed and they are not specially rare. Nevertheless, so many collectors want an example of the first stamp of all that ones in good condition are worth quite a lot (about £2,500 or US$4,500 unused and about £150 or US$270 used).

Twopenny Blues came into use a few days after the Penny Blacks and remained in use for 40 years, with three slight changes to the design. The original Twopenny Blues are rarer than Penny Blacks and worth about twice as much, though the other three versions are worth a lot less. Neither Penny Blacks nor Twopenny Blues were perforated, so they had to be cut apart.

The mark used to cancel Penny Blacks and Twopenny Blues was a red Maltese cross. This usually fell on the centre of the stamp, unlike modern cancellations, which surround it or fall to one side. It was possible to wash the red cross off and use the stamp again, so the colour was changed to black. Then it no longer showed up on the black stamp so, in 1841, the Penny Black was withdrawn.

The Penny Black was replaced by the Penny Red (described in catalogues as being brown in colour). Like Twopenny Blues, these stayed in use until 1880, with a few minor changes to the design. Perforations were introduced and numbers began to be printed in the borders of the stamps to show which plate had been used to print them. Some Penny Reds are very valuable.

The next place to issue stamps was the region of Zurich, in Switzerland, in 1843. Soon after, two other Swiss regions (Geneva and Basel) also issued stamps.

After Zurich, the next place to issue stamps was Brazil, also in 1843. These first Brazilian stamps are known as "Bull's-eyes" and some are quite valuable.

The next country to issue stamps was the U.S.A. This 5 cent stamp of Benjamin Franklin and a 10 cent stamp of George Washington were issued in 1847.

The next stamps were issued by Mauritius, also in 1847. The first 500 each of the penny and twopenny stamps to be printed read "post office" instead of "post paid". This was altered for later printings, but the few originals that survived are now worth several hundred thousand pounds each.

## Stamps on stamps

Almost all the earliest stamps are far too rare and expensive for ordinary collectors ever to acquire, but many stamps have been issued which show the old stamps on them and it is quite possible to build up a worthwhile thematic collection of these. Many of the stamps show the Penny Black and Rowland Hill, who introduced it, together with the first stamp of the issuing country.

# 1 Changes in design

Pictorial issued in 1910.     Commemorative issued in 1898.

Stamps were an immediate success, both commercially and with collectors, and designers soon started looking for new ideas for subjects. In the late 1800s and early 1900s the first true pictorials and commemoratives were produced.

## The first odd-shaped stamp

The first stamp which was not either square or rectangular was this one, issued in 1853 by the Cape of Good Hope. It was made triangular in shape so that it would be recognized easily and letters could be sorted quickly.

## The U.P.U.

Symbol of the U.P.U.

It used to be quite complicated for letters to cross country boundaries, but in 1874 the Universal Postal Union (U.P.U.) was founded and all the member countries agreed to accept each other's stamps on incoming mail. The U.P.U. is still responsible for organizing international co-operation between countries with postal services. Every new stamp has to be submitted to the U.P.U. so that it has an up-to-date record of genuine stamps. Look out for the U.P.U. symbol, especially on stamps issued to commemorate the postal services.

# 2

Canada 1928     Canada 1977

Austria 1916     Austria 1973

Most early stamps showed things like the country's ruler, its coat of arms, mythological figures, something symbolic (a post-horn for example) or just numbers. Even today, though more and more countries are issuing

## Key plates

Countries which had colonies often used to print stamps with identical designs for all of them, using "key" plates. Only the different place names and values were printed separately. Here are some stamps printed in the early 1900s for British colonies.

## The most famous rare stamp

There is only one known surviving example of a number of stamps but this one, issued by British Guiana (now Guyana) in 1856, is the most famous. It was found in 1873 by a 12-year-old boy, who sold it for six shillings (30p). In 1980 it was sold for US$850,000 (about £400,000). In proportion to its size and weight, it is probably the most valuable single object in the world.

France 1906     France 1977

Belgium 1883     Belgium 1977

definitives illustrating other things (for example, the Austrian landscape and Canadian flower stamps above), many are still based on traditional designs. Here are some old and new definitives for you to compare.

## Early collections

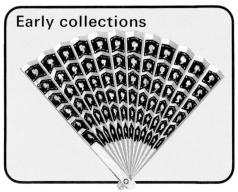

People collected stamps from the time they first appeared but they had no idea they might become valuable and did not keep them in good condition. Thousands of Penny Blacks were used to decorate fans and vases.

## What makes a stamp valuable?

If a lot of people want a stamp which is in short supply, the value of the stamp increases.

Except for very old and rare stamps, stamps have to be in good condition to be valuable. This is a point to bear in mind if you hope to sell your own collection one day. Remember, though, that good condition does not necessarily mean mint.

It is never possible to know for certain which stamps will increase in value. On the whole, it is a good idea to buy sets of current stamps which are only going to be available for a limited time. Any specialized collection in good condition is a sound investment.

# Air and sea mail

Some collectors like to specialize in mail that has travelled by air or sea. This can be quite expensive but you might come across some of the types of things shown on these two pages, so it is worth looking out for them. Air and sea mail envelopes often have a lot of interesting information on them. Some early ones even show the name of the plane or ship which carried them. Don't cut up air and sea mail envelopes, especially the old ones, or you will reduce their value.

If you want to specialize in air mail, you can collect not only stamps but also air mail stationery and labels, and first flight covers.

## Air mail stamps

Several countries issue special air mail stamps. Large countries which send some of their internal mail by air sometimes used to issue separate stamps for internal air mail and air mail going abroad. If you get any of these, try and keep them separate from your general air mail stamps. Some of these are shown on page 4.

External air mail

Internal air mail

## Air mail labels

Air mail labels are usually blue and have the French words, *par avion*, on them, with the equivalent in the national language. You could mount them in your album in alphabetical order of country but it is best to keep them on a separate page from your stamps. Always remember never to cut up an interesting envelope.

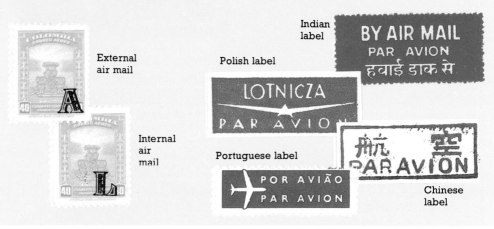

Indian label

Polish label

Portuguese label

Chinese label

## Paquebot letters

The word *paquebot* appears on a lot of letters that were posted at sea in the early 1900s. In the 1890s the countries in the Universal Postal Union decided that this French word, meaning "packet boat", should be incorporated into the postmarks of all letters posted on board ships. The letter below travelled from Jamaica to London via the port of Bristol, where it was postmarked. Notice how this letter also has "ocean mail" on it. *Paquebot* still appears on some letters sent by sea today.

## First voyage covers

Before the days of the aeroplane, all overseas mail had to go by sea.

Until quite recently, special envelopes were often produced to commemorate the maiden voyages of important ships which would carry mail.

These were postmarked before being taken on board, like the one above, or, if they were posted at sea, at the port of arrival. First voyage covers are less rare than first flight covers and are fairly easy and cheap to buy.

## Pigeon post

Before people had telephones or could send telegrams, pigeons were sometimes used to carry letters quickly and special stamps were issued for pigeon mail. This one was for the service which operated between Herm and Guernsey in the Channel Islands. Lightweight letter sheets carried by pigeons are known as "pigeongrams". Pigeon post is still used occasionally as a gimmick.

## First flight covers

These are special envelopes which were produced to be carried on pioneer flights or, like the one above, to commemorate the opening of a new air mail route. A lot of regular services were set up in the 1920s and 1930s and nowadays more mail goes by air than by sea. First flight covers are quite rare.

## Rocket post

There have been many experiments at sending mail by rocket, especially in India and the U.S.A. This stamp was issued for some experimental flights which were made in Scotland, between the islands of Scarp and Harris. Rocket mail stamps are not very expensive to buy. Nowadays rocket mail is only used as a gimmick.

## Wreck covers

These are envelopes salvaged from shipwrecks. The one below was recovered from the water after the flying boat carrying it from Papua to England crashed into the sea off ▼ Greece in 1936. Wreck covers are almost always damaged, and sometimes have their stamps washed right off, but because they are rare and in demand, this does not reduce their value.

▲
## Early sea mail

A lot of letters used to be carried on private ships and the postage included a small fee to the captain. The mail had either the stamps of the country from which it was sent or, if it was posted on board, stamps of the country of origin of the ship. It was usually postmarked at the first port of call in the country of its destination. This letter was posted on a British ship sailing from Gibraltar to Liverpool, England. Look out for old envelopes which have "ship letter" or the equivalent in a foreign language on them. Many are now rare and valuable, including this one.

# Identifying stamps

It is sometimes difficult to know where a stamp is from if the country name on it is completely different from the English translation. This makes it hard to know where to look the stamp up in catalogues, which list stamps under their country of origin.

Below is a list of names and key words which appear on stamps, together with the English equivalent. The word on the left is the one on the stamps, the word on the right is the one to look up in the catalogue.

If you still can't find the country in the catalogue, it may be because it is, or used to be, the colony or possession of another country and is listed at the end of that country's entry. Similarly, if a country has become part of another one, it may be listed at the end of that country.

The best way of locating difficult stamps is to look first in a general world catalogue (such as Stanley Gibbons, *Stamps of the World*), where the countries are more likely to appear in strict alphabetical order. At the beginning of the entry you will be given some information about the country and you will then have a better idea of where to look for it in a specialized catalogue if you want more details about the stamps.

Açores: Azores
Afghanes: Afghanistan
Africa Occidental Española: Spanish West Africa
Africa Orientale Italiana: Italian East Africa
Afrique Equatoriale Française: French Equatoriale Africa
Afrique Occidentale Française: French West Africa
Algérie or Algérienne: Algeria
Andorre: Andorra
Arabie Sauodite: Saudi Arabia

Bayern: Bavaria
Belgie or Belgique: Belgium
Belgisch Congo: Belgian Congo
Böhmen und Mähren: Bohemia and Moravia
Brasil: Brazil
Braunschweig: Brunswick

Cabo Verde: Cape Verde Islands
Cambodge: Cambodia
CCCP: Russia
Centrafricain: Central African Empire
Centrafricaine: Central African Republic
Ceskoslovensko: Czechoslovakia
Comores or Comorien: Comoro Islands
Congo Belge: Belgian Congo
Côte d'Ivoire: Ivory Coast
Côte Française des Somalis: French Somali Coast

Danmark: Denmark
DDR: Germany (East)
Deutsche Bundespost: Germany (West)
Deutsche Demokratische Republik: Germany (East)
Deutsche Post: Germany
Deutsches Reich: Germany
Dominicana: Dominican Republic

Eesti: Estonia
Égypte or Égyptienne: Egypt
Eire: Ireland (Republic)
España or Española: Spain
Établissements Français de l'Océanie: Oceanic Settlements

Établissements Français dans l'Inde: French Indian Settlements
Éthiopie: Ethiopia

Føroyar: Faroe Islands
Française: France

Gabonaise: Gabon
Grønland: Greenland
Guinea Ecuatorial: Equatorial Guinea
Guinea España or Española: Spanish Guinea
Guinée: Guinea
Guinée Bissau: Guinea Bissau
Guinée Française: French Guinea
Guiné Portuguesa: Portuguese Guinea
Guyane Française: French Guiana

Haute Silésie: Upper Silesia
Haute Volta: Upper Volta
Hellas: Greece
Helvetia: Switzerland

India Portuguesa: Portuguese India
Indochine: Indo-China
Island: Iceland
Italia, Italiana or Italiane: Italy

Jugoslavija: Yugoslavia

Khmere: Khmer Republic
Kibris: Cyprus
KSA: Saudi Arabia

LAR: Libya
Latvija: Latvia
Liban or Libanaise: Lebanon
Lietuva: Lithuania

Macau: Macao
Magyar: Hungary
Magyarorszag: Hungary
Malgache: Malagasy Republic
Maroc: Morocco
Marruecos: Morocco or Spanish Morocco
Mauritanie: Mauritania
Melayu: Malayan Federation
Moçambique: Mozambique
Moyen-Congo: Middle Congo

Nederland: Netherlands

Nederlandsch-Indië or Ned Indië: Netherlands Indies
Nederlandse Antillen: Netherlands Antilles
Nippon: Japan
Norge: Norway
Nouvelle Calédonie: New Caledonia

Österreich or Österreichisch: Austria

PDR Yemen: Yemen People's Democratic Republic
Persanes: Iran
Pilipinas: Philippines
Polska: Poland
Polynésie Française: French Polynesia
Portuguesa: Portugal
Preussen: Prussia
Pulau Pinang: Penang

Reichspost: Germany
RF: France
Romana: Romania
R P Romina: Romania
RSA: South Africa
Rwandaise: Rwanda

SA: Saudi Arabia
Sachsen: Saxony
Sahara España or Español: Spanish Sahara
Salvador: El Salvador
São Tomé e Príncipe: St Thomas and Prince Island
Saurashtra: Soruth
Shqipenie, Shqipni, Shqiperia, Shqiperise, Shqyptare: Albania
Siam: Thailand
Slovensko: Slovakia
S. Marino: San Marino
Soudan Français: French Sudan
S. Tomé e Príncipe: St Thomas and Prince Island
STT Vuja: Trieste
Suid-Afrika: South Africa
Suidwes-Afrika: South West Africa
Suomi: Finland
Suriname: Surinam
Sverige: Sweden
SWA: South West Africa
Syrie or Syrienne: Syria

*Remember, British stamps do not have a country name on them – just the monarch's head.*

Tchad: Chad
Terres Australes et Antarctiques
   Françaises: French Southern and
   Antarctic Territories
Territoire Français des Afars et des
   Issas: French Territory of the Afars
   and the Issas
Toga: Tonga
Togolaise: Togo
Touva: Tuva
Tripoli: Tripolitania
Tunisie or Tunisienne: Tunisia
Türkiye: Turkey

UAE: United Arab Emirates
UAR: Egypt or Syria
US: United States of America

Vaticane: Vatican City
Viet-nam Cong-Hoa: South Vietnam
Viet-nam Dan Chu Cong Hoa: North
   Vietnam

YAR: Yemen Arab Republic

Z. Afr. Republiek: Transvaal

If the name on the stamp is in a completely different alphabet from ours, it can be especially difficult to tell where the stamp is from. Here are some unusual names that you will come across.

| | |
|---|---|
| ΕΛΛΑΣ | Greece |
| 日本郵便 | Japan |
| БЪЛГАРИЯ | Bulgaria |
| МОНГОЛ ШУУДАН | Mongolia |
| 中国人民邮政 | China |
| 朝鮮郵票 | North Korea |
| 票郵國民華中 | China (Taiwan) |
| ПОЧТА | Russia |
| КРНТН | Crete |
| СРБИЈА | Serbia |
| HRVATSKA | Croatia |
| СН 한민국우표 | South Korea |
| ΚΥΠΡΟΣ | Cyprus |
| ЈУГОСЛАВИЈА | Yugoslavia |

## Using a catalogue

You can find out a lot about individual stamps by looking them up in a catalogue. These are really dealers' price lists but the main ones give details of every stamp ever issued and so are useful reference books. Stanley Gibbons in Britain and Scott in the U.S.A. issue general world catalogues and also shorter, specialized ones with one or more countries in each. The stamps are listed under the name of the issuing country in date order.

Catalogues are expensive to buy, though you can often get last year's edition at a reduced price. Public and stamp club libraries will have catalogues you can use if you don't want to buy one.

Catalogues look quite complicated at first, but once you get used to them, they are not difficult to follow. First, look up the country of origin of your stamp. Then look through the entries under that country. There is not room for a picture of every stamp

but one from each set is usually shown and those that are not pictured are described.

If your stamp is not in the catalogue, it may not be an ordinary postage stamp, but a special purpose stamp, a local or privately issued stamp or even a bogus one. Some catalogues list these at the end of a country's entries, so check there. If you can't find a stamp in any of the catalogues, ask a more experienced collector if they can help you.

This extract shows you the kind of information you will find in one of the more comprehensive types of catalogue. The entries for the two sets of stamps shown here are from *Stanley Gibbons Stamp Catalogue (Part 7)*.

Design type number.

Purpose of issue.

Date of issue.

Stamp number (allocated to stamp by catalogue publishers).

Denomination. (These are charity stamps, so the surcharge is shown too.)

Figures in bold type refer to picture above.

Miniature sheet.

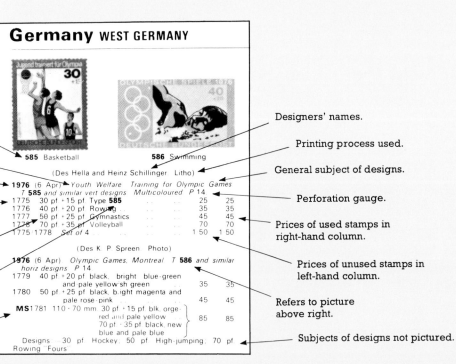

Designers' names.

Printing process used.

General subject of designs.

Perforation gauge.

Prices of used stamps in right-hand column.

Prices of unused stamps in left-hand column.

Refers to picture above right.

Subjects of designs not pictured.

# Stamp words

When you first start collecting stamps, you will hear lots of technical words you don't understand. Here is a list of some of the words you might come across. The most common stamp words have been explained earlier in this book, so if the word you want is not in this list, try looking it up in the index.

**Adhesive:** a gummed stamp as opposed to one printed on postal stationery.

**Aerogramme:** a lightweight letter sheet for sending air mail, often with a stamp printed on it.

**Block:** four or more unseparated stamps, other than in a strip.

**Bogus:** a stamp which is not genuine.

**Cancellation:** a postmark applied to a stamp to show it has been through the post and cannot be reused.

**Changeling:** a stamp whose colour has changed, often in sunlight or water.

**Cinderella philately:** the collection of local or privately issued stamps, fiscals, labels and bogus stamps.

**Classic:** an early stamp, usually one issued before 1875.

**Commemorative:** a stamp issued to celebrate a special event or anniversary.

**Corner block:** a block of stamps from the corner of a sheet.

**Cover:** an envelope. Used stamps on an envelope are said to be "on cover". A first day cover is one postmarked on the first day of issue of the stamps it bears.

**Definitive:** a normal, "everyday" stamp of a country.

**Demonitized:** obsolete stamps which are no longer valid to pay postage.

**Denomination:** the postal value printed on a stamp.

**Error:** a stamp which has a mistake in its design, printing or perforation.

**Essay:** a suggested design for a stamp.

**Fake:** a stamp which has been altered to make it look like a more valuable one; also a damaged stamp which has been repaired.

**Fiscal:** a stamp used to show payment of things other than postage, such as taxes, licence or court fees.

**Flaw:** a mark or blemish on a stamp, often caused by a damaged printing plate or cylinder.

**Forgery:** an illegally printed imitation of a real stamp.

**Frank:** a mark to show that postage either has been paid or need not be paid.

**Gutter:** the space between two panes of a sheet of stamps. A gutter pair is two stamps with a gutter between them.

**Handstamp:** a postmark applied by hand, not by machine.

**Imperforate:** a stamp without perforations.

**Invert:** a stamp with part of the design accidentally printed upside down.

**Issue:** a number of related stamps produced and put on sale at the same time.

A gutter pair

A fiscal stamp

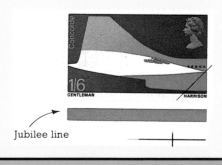

Jubilee line

# Going further

## Local clubs

It is a good idea to join a stamp club. You will meet other people who are interested in your hobby, including more experienced collectors who can advise you, and you will be able to borrow books and catalogues, find out about exhibitions and competitions, and arrange to swap stamps. Most towns have clubs and almost all offer junior membership at a special, low rate. You should be able to get the address of the nearest club from your local library.

## National clubs

You can belong to these as well as to a local club, as long as you can afford both subscriptions. The largest in Britain is the National Philatelic Society (1 Whitehall Place, London SW1A 2HE). The largest in the U.S.A. is the American Philatelic Society Inc. (P.O. Box 800, State College, PA 16801, U.S.A.). The American Topical Association (3306 North 50th Street, Milwaukee, Wisconsin 53216, U.S.A.) is useful to thematic collectors. All three clubs have members all over the world. Always remember to include an international reply coupon if you are writing to a club abroad.

## Magazines

These are very useful, especially for the advertisements which tell you what the dealers have for sale and where and when exhibitions and auctions are taking place.
*Great Britain:*
Gibbons Stamp Monthly
Philatelic Magazine (monthly)
Stamp Collecting (weekly)
Stamp Magazine (monthly)
Stamps (monthly)
*U.S.A.:*
The American Philatelist (monthly)
Linn's Weekly Stamp News
Mekeel's Weekly Stamp News
Stamps (weekly)
Western Stamp Collector (twice weekly)
*Australia:*
Australian Stamp Monthly
Stamp News (monthly)
Stamp Preview (newsletter)

Jubilee line: a coloured line round the edge of a sheet of stamps.

Kiloware: mixtures of used stamps sold by weight.

Mint: an unused stamp in perfect condition.

Multiple: three or more unseparated stamps.

Obliteration: a type of cancellation, intended to blot out the stamp.

Obsolete: a stamp which is no longer on sale at the post office but may still be valid for postage.

Omnibus issue: stamps issued by several countries at once to commemorate the same event, often with the same or similar design.

Pane: a section of a sheet of stamps, separated from other sections by a gutter; also, a small sheet of stamps in a booklet.

Pair: two unseparated stamps.

Perforations: the lines of small holes punched between stamps so they can be torn apart.

Phantom stamps: see bogus.

Pictorial: any stamp with a picture on it.

Plate: a piece of metal with the stamp design on it from which stamps are printed.

Postal stationery: envelopes, postcards or other wrappers which have stamps printed on them.

Postmark: an official mark applied to a letter to show it has been through the post.

Proofs: stamps printed on a trial run before full production begins.

Provisionals: stamps in use temporarily until new ones are ready.

Remainders: stocks left over at the post office when a stamp becomes obsolete. Remainders are sometimes sold off cheaply to dealers.

Rouletting: a type of perforation in which slits, not holes, are made between stamps.

Revenue stamps: see fiscals.

Set: a number of related stamps issued in a series of denominations at the same time or over a period.

Se-tenant: two or more stamps of a different colour, denomination or design joined together.

Sheet: Stamps come off the printing machine in sheets, which are usually divided into four panes, or in a roll which is later cut into sheets.

Strip: three or more stamps joined together in a single row, either horizontal or vertical.

Tête-bêche: a pair of unseparated stamps of which one is upside down in relation to the other.

Unused: a stamp which has not been through the post but is not in perfect condition.

Used: a stamp which has been through the post.

Variety: a stamp which is slightly different from most of the others in a batch, due to a fault during printing.

Watermark: a pattern pressed into some stamp paper during production as a precaution against forgery.

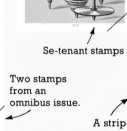

Se-tenant stamps

Two stamps from an omnibus issue.

A strip

A tête-bêche pair

## Books

The most useful books for beginners are Stanley Gibbons series of guides, which are quite cheap, and the American Topical Association's series of booklets on various themes.

## Catalogues

Stanley Gibbons, Great Britain, and J. Walter Scott, U.S.A., publish general and specialized catalogues which are used throughout the English speaking world. You should be able to find them in a library. You may also come across catalogues by Minkus, U.S.A., Yvert et Tellier, France, and Michel, Germany.

## Dealers

Look in the philatelic magazines for stamp dealers' advertisements. Or ask to see a directory of dealers in a library. These are published by the Philatelic Trader's Society in Britain, the American Stamp Dealer's Association in the U.S.A. and the Australasian Stamp Dealers' Association in Australia.

## Philatelic bureaux

Most countries have a philatelic bureau from which you can buy current, and sometimes past, issues. The bureaux advertise in the philatelic magazines. If you fill in and send off the printed coupon which almost always appears with the advertisement, they will send you information about what is available and how you can order by post. Many bureaux also have counters in major post offices.

## Exhibitions

Major exhibitions are advertised in the philatelic magazines. Smaller exhibitions are arranged by local clubs. The rules which govern the exhibitors and the judges are laid down by the Fédération Internationale de Philatelie.

## Important museums

*Great Britain:*
The National Postal Museum, London
The British Library, London
*U.S.A.:*
The Smithsonian Institute, Washington
*Canada:*
The National Postal Museum, Ottawa.

# Index

Printed in Hong Kong / China

First Published in 1981 by Usborne Publishing Ltd, Usborne House, 83-87 Saffron Hill, London EC1N 8RT, England.
Copyright © 1981 Usborne Publishing Ltd.

This edition Published in 1998 by Tiger Books International PLC, Twickenham, U.K.

ISBN 1-84056-005-3

We should like to thank the following for lending us stamps, covers and transparencies for use in this book:; National Postal Museum, London, Douglas Muir, Harry Dagnall, J.A.L. Franks Ltd, Stanley Gibbons Auctions Ltd, Stanley Newham, Royale Stamps Co., Kenneth S. Sargeant and Wiggins Teape Group Ltd.